I0414877

U! GET THAT MONKEY
OFF YOUR OWN BACK!

By: Nathaniel E. Mason

First published in 1995 by Choices, Post Office Box 152, Chester, Pa. 19013

ISBN: 0-7596-4084-X

This book is printed on acid free paper.

Unless otherwise noted, all scripture taken from the King James Version of the Bible.

First Printing 1998

International Standard Book Number 0-9665983-0-X

Library of Congress Card Number 98-72993

Printed in the United States of America

1stBooks – rev. 06/01/01

ACKNOWLEDGMENT

This book was inspired by a number of factors, but most notably, God and my big sister Earline. To both I say thanks.

TABLE OF CONTENTS

INTRODUCTION

"U!...GET THAT MONKEY OFF YOUR OWN BACK!" was written to try and help **YOU** rid yourself of unwanted tendencies, or "bad" habits. It uses a commonsense approach in its attempt to help you do so. You will see as you read on that a lot of this book sounds familiar. It attempts to get you to use what you, more than likely, already know. Though I must say, **what you know in your head and what you know in your heart are sometimes two different things.** For instance, a smoker may know in their head that smoking is bad for their health, but until they know it in their heart, they'll never stop smoking.

This book also offers some spiritual guidance. Its' goal is to help you, by getting you to look at things from a different perspective. The way you see things effects the way you react to those things. For example: the sight of blood. Most people can't watch a surgeon operate because of the sight of blood. It makes them feel very uncomfortable. A surgeon probably couldn't be a surgeon without seeing some blood. He or she probably sees this spilled blood much like a mechanic sees spilled motor oil or transmission fluid. I would have to say that most people don't cringe or would want to vomit from the sight of spilled motor oil or transmission fluid. So you see, **your perspective**, the way

you see things, will definitely effect the way **you react** to those things.

This book is not intended to be long winded or drawn out, but straight and to the point. Besides, you don't need five hundred pages and twelve audiotapes to change your life. I'd doubt you'd have the time to sit down and memorize all that information anyway. Even in this book you'd have to spend some amount of time to commit everything to memory. That's not the objective. My recommendation is that you pick out and highlight the words, phrases, or paragraphs, (that aren't already highlighted) from each chapter that strikes a nerve with you. Memorize these and begin to incorporate them into your daily life. Little by little, if you'll stick with them, they'll become second nature to you. You'll do them without even thinking about it. And at this point that monkey (bad habit) will be long gone.

Think About It!

SELF-IMPORTANCE

In order to deal with life's problems without becoming depressed or developing a crutch, you must be important to **YOURSELF.** Most people who remain in abusive relationships have very low self-esteem, or self worth. They feel that they somehow deserve the treatment they're receiving. Most people that abuse their bodies through drugs, alcohol, perversion, etc. have some degree of low self worth. Why else would you knowingly destroy your own body? **You're the only you that you've got.** Most people who commit suicide have lost all self worth. They feel that they're failures for some reason or another. They think that there's absolutely no way out of their trouble. (Which by the way, is a lie.) They don't know the immediate answer to their problem, so they decide upon death as their only way of escape.

You are a unique creature. Not only are you able to adapt to different situations, you're able to create and grow. Think about an apple seed. This little, seemingly insignificant, morsel has within it the potential to become something far greater than it ever started out as. Over time it could literally feed millions. Well guess what? You have an even greater potential. Because not only can you grow, you can adapt and create while doing it. How many times have you seen an apple tree come in out of the

1

storm, or suddenly start-producing oranges? Never. **But you on the other hand can do anything you set your mind to.** You are an extremely unique creature.

You are part of the human race. The highest form of creation on this entire planet, believe it or not. There is not another human being on the face of this earth exactly like you and there never will be. Nobody looks exactly like you. (Not even your identical twin.) Nobody walks, talks, writes, imagines, or does anything else you can think of, exactly like you. **You're one of a kind. Priceless!** More rare and valuable than the largest and most brilliantly cut diamond. In fact, without humankind, the diamonds, rubies, pearls, gold, silver, and any other precious commodity would be absolutely worthless.

Imagine if you will that you're on a nature hike out in the woods. Suddenly you notice a dark hole in the side of a hill up ahead. It's a cave. Being the adventurer that you are, you decide to go in and have a look. As soon as you get inside, you flick on your flashlight. The light beam cuts through the darkness creating a spotlight on the cave wall. You soon hear what sounds like tree leaves blowing in a summer breeze. The sound is coming from above so you shine your light on the cave ceiling. You're shocked to see that the sounds you've heard were not being made by leaves at all, but by the leathery wings of the thousands of irritated bats that cover the cave ceiling. They immediately drop from their perches and take flight, heading for the cave door. Without a second to spare before you've got a face full of bats, you dive to the cave floor. Your flashlight flies from your hand, hits the cave floor, and rolls to a stop about ten feet away. You scramble to your feet and head for the flashlight with one thing in mind; "I'm getting out of here...Fast!" Just before you grab your flashlight and begin your sprint to daylight, you notice the beam is gleaning off several objects scattered amongst the rocks. This captures your curiosity, and suddenly the thought of escaping is null and void. You walk over to examine these shimmering objects and soon discover that you've literally stumbled on to a horde of precious stones and gold nuggets. Needless to say, you're overcome with joy, for you are now what some call "filthy rich."

The point of this little imaginative exercise is this; No matter how many precious stones or gold nuggets were in that cave, none of it had a value until **you** discovered it. You gave the gold and precious stones value. The bats surely weren't concerned about it. It was just another part of the cave to them. There could be a monkey in some jungle right now using the world's largest uncut diamond to open coconuts or something. To him it's a rock. If it doesn't work too well, he'll throw it away and get another rock. To you or I it's untold riches. But it doesn't have a value until a human being gets their hands on it. **We give it value, not vice versa.** Furthermore, think about how you'd take care of a Rolls Royce automobile, ten-caret diamond, or a beautiful mansion. You wouldn't neglect or trash them. You'd treat them with the utmost care. Why? Because they're very valuable objects. Yet and still, that's all they are are objects. They don't give birth, perform life saving surgery, or give good advice. We do. So you need to start treating yourself as well as you'd treat a car, a rock, a home, or anything else of "value."

You need to think of yourself as important. Very important. Simply because you are. It doesn't matter how you look, how much money you have, or what other people may think of you. If you can give value to the most precious "objects" known to mankind, then I'd say that makes you even more valuable and more precious. In fact, anything on the face of this earth that has a value, be it land, money, or a bag of fertilizer, humankind has placed the value on that item. So remember, you, me, and everyone else on this planet are absolutely priceless. **There is not a monetary value that can justifiably be put on a human life.** Each one of us is a work of art, a one of a kind masterpiece. We're only here on this earth for a short time, and when we're gone there will never be another one exactly like us. So stand tall and be strong!

Get in front of a mirror, look yourself straight in the eyes and say; "I am important, very important, because I am priceless!"

Think about it!

SELF-CONFIDENCE

The dictionary defines self-confidence as; "The belief in ones own abilities." This is not to be confused with ego because ego is strictly self-serving. You wouldn't be egotistical about someone else, but you are sometimes confident in someone else. The big difference between ego and confidence is that your ego is easily hurt. Confidence may get knocked down, but it **always** gets back up and resumes the quest.

Let's say you have an egotistical boxer fighting a self confident one. The egotistical boxer is the champ with a record of fifty wins, no losses, no ties, and all fifty wins by knockout. He's loud and he's proud. The self-confident boxer is a newcomer. He has a record of five wins, two losses, one tie, and one win by knockout.

Ding! Ding! The bell rings and they come out fighting. The egotistical fighter is bouncing around, loudly telling his opponent what he's going to do to him. See, he must be seen and heard. He must be the center of attention. Meanwhile, the confident boxer is quietly and methodically feeling out his opponent, searching for the right moment to strike. **POW!** The egotistical fighter just hit his opponent with a bone crushing right cross to the head, knocking him flat on his back. As he jumps around the ring proclaiming his greatness, he notices something that causes him a hint of concern; the confident fighter is getting up. "He can't be!" he thinks, "I hit him with everything I had! Nobody else ever got up after I hit 'em that hard."

Yet, the confident fighter comes forward. The egotistical fighter reminds him of how hard he was just hit and where he just lay, but to no avail. The confident fighter doesn't bat an eye. He just continues his stalk, thinking; "Okay. He caught me with a good one there. I underestimated him. But I'll guarantee you I won't make that same mistake again. The next time he throws a punch, I'll be ready." The egotistical fighter does just that, launching a fierce right "haymaker" aimed at his opponent's head. This time the confident fighter quickly ducks out of harms way and comes back up with a devastating left hook of his own. It lands square on the chin of the egotistical fighter, sending him rocking and reeling back to the ropes where he falls out flat on his face. As he lay there taking the count, he wonders what the crowd must be thinking. He decides not to get up. Not because he's physically unable to continue, but because he's embarrassed. He can't believe he let another fighter knock him down, flat on his face even. That's absolutely unheard of. He'd prefer to take the ten count, get up and get out of there as fast as humanly possible. This, to him, is a much safer choice than taking a chance of being embarrassed even further by yet another knockdown. The confident fighter wins!

Confidence will always win in the long run. Because confidence remains focused on its goal. It may be knocked down a hundred times. But with each knockdown a new lesson is learned. Confidence gets back up and moves toward its goal, knowing one more mistake not to make. **Ego**, on the other hand, is very busy loudly proclaiming its greatness, trying terribly hard to convince everyone around it that the words it speaks are true. When it does get knocked down, or suffer some kind of loss, it's so concerned with what people will think, that it must run and hide until the embarrassment goes away.

I say to you, be confident, not egotistical. Egotism is to think too highly of yourself. As if you're somehow better than everyone else is. **You're no better than anyone else is, but by no means is anyone else better than you are.** I'm not talking about God given talents here. Sure, there are individuals who are better at doing certain things than other individuals. For instance, someone may have a natural talent for sports, while someone else may have a natural talent for math, while still someone else may have a natural talent for art. The list could go on and on. These talents are not what I'm talking about. I'm talking about we, as human beings are no better than each other. You know how some people think that they are somehow better than other people, based solely on the color of their skin? What idiotic thinking this is. Nothing could be further from the truth.

It's like saying; "I own a blue Rolls Royce and you own a green one, therefore mine is better than yours just because it's blue." Can you see how utterly preposterous this is?

Let's say we take two people from different races that absolutely hate each other because of their respective races, and put them on opposite sides of a deserted island. I'll guarantee you that after a while these two will begin to communicate. And before long they'll become friends. You know why? Because as the old saying goes; "No man is an island." I don't care how much of a loner you are. I don't care how much of a nature lover you are. You can't communicate with the plants and animals on your level. Sure, you can love your plants and you can love your animals. But you can't sit down and have an in depth two way conversation with them. You can't ask them for advice. You can't teach them algebra or trigonometry. And you sure can't make love to them (at least not if you're in your right mind). So you see, this thing about a certain race being better than another race is a lie. **We all belong to the human race.** If two humans of two different ethnicities have a child, they produce just that, a human child. They don't produce a horse, a bird, or a tree. They produce after their kind. Just as a horse produces more horses, a bird produces more birds, and a tree produces more trees. If we as humans don't get along, it's not because we can't; it's because we **choose** not to.

I truly believe that if there were some long list of every human talent and or behavior, and each individual got a point for any area that he or she was strong in and a point taken away for any area that he or she was weak in, all our total scores would add up to be a big fat zero. What I mean is, **we - as humans - are all - on the same level.** Once you realize this, you won't have any problems with self-confidence. You'll know beyond the shadow of a doubt that anyone you've ever encountered, or ever will, is no more, or less, human than you. I know there are people who think they're better than others for any number of reasons, but I'm here to tell you they aren't. Why? Because all humans are conceived the same way (sperm meets egg). All humans need food, drink, and shelter. All humans have the same body parts, and all of those body parts work exactly the same way no matter what color they are. All humans reside on this same planet earth. All humans live, and all humans die. All humans have strengths, and all humans have weaknesses. **All humans!** I don't care how famous, how rich, how attractive, or how smart, if they're human then they're no better or worse than you or I.

Let's say you take two people. You and I for example. Let's say you're good at math and I'm not. Math would be a strength for you and a weakness for me. Then on the other hand I could be a great artist, while your creative skills are poor at best. Again, this would be a strength, this time for me, and a weakness, this time for you. The list could go on and on. The point being is; we all have areas of our lives that come fairly easy to us (strengths), and areas that we find difficult to grasp (weaknesses). It doesn't make me better than you or vice versa. It just means we're different. We both have to go to work honing our strengths and controlling or overcoming our weaknesses. Remember this; **"A weakness that is overcome, with practice, can become a strength."** You know why? Because we all have relatively the same size brain. And if your brain is healthy and functioning as it should, then you have the ability to learn. Haven't you ever heard the saying; "You're not stupid. You just don't know." Think of how true this statement is. You're not a brain surgeon, not because you're too stupid to be one, but because you've never trained to be one. And I believe if you took any ordinary person, with or without a college degree, and let them apprentice with a brain surgeon day in and day out, sooner or later they'll know brain surgery too. I'm sure you've heard people say they could never learn to do some thing. Well, if this is what they say, and this is what they believe, then guess what? This is what they'll get. They'll never learn to do that thing. Self-confidence always says; "I can and I will!" Sure, it may take you a little longer than someone else to

11

learn or do a specific thing. But so what? **If you'll continue to believe, you'll eventually achieve.**

Believe in your own abilities! Believe in yourself, and never ever be anyone's doormat. **You were not put on this earth to be walked all over by a bunch of insensitive jerks.** Believe me, misery loves company. And if you're around some insensitive miserable person or persons, they'll more than likely try to make you as miserable as they are. Don't accept that invitation to the misery ball. Instead, demand respect by respecting yourself. Hold your head up high and walk tall in confidence.

Did you know that **no one could make you believe anything but you? (You'll believe you before you'll believe anyone else.)** Let's say you're sitting at your desk doodling one day, when suddenly you get an idea for a better mousetrap. You make a sketch up and decide to show it to your best friend. When they see it, immediately they get excited and tell you what a great idea it is. They go on to offer you any help you might need in bringing this product to market. You reply by saying; "I was just kidding. This thing will never sell. Thanks, but no thanks." You have just believed yourself. You doubted, and you believed your doubts.

Now on the other hand, your friend could be totally against your idea. They might think it's a piece of crap. And you might say; "I'll show you. This thing will sell. It'll sell like hotcakes! Just you wait and see!" In both cases you believed you. This is always the case, no matter what the situation. You've heard the phrase; "They made a believer out of me." No they didn't. They presented something to you. You analyzed and evaluated it, and then you decided to believe it. They didn't make you believe anything. So if you're going to be a confident person it's going to ultimately have to be you who believes in you. It doesn't matter what your spouse, your mom, your best friend, or even your kids, believe. **The only thing that's gonna effect your behavior is what you believe. (You'll only act on what you believe.)** You know why? Because you know you better than anyone else on this planet ever will. You've heard the expression; "You can't escape yourself because everywhere you go there you are." How true. How true. You live with you twenty-four hours a day, seven days a week, three hundred and sixty five and one quarter days a year. No one knows your thoughts but you. No one knows your next action but you.

You should never let another persons' opinion define you, whether good or bad. You have to define yourself. For instance, let's say someone calls you a lazy bum. It could be someone you don't know, or it could be someone very close to you. It doesn't matter. Right away you have two choices. You can believe it and accept it as a definition of yourself, or you can disbelieve it and reject it as a lie. **The choice is yours and yours alone.** If you believe something that someone says about you solely on the basis that it was this someone who said it, so it must be true, then something is very wrong. Remember, absolutely no one knows you better than you do. And we as human beings have the ability to change our minds in the blink of an eye. A person could be a lazy bum their entire life, then one moment of one day they decide they aren't going to be a lazy bum anymore. The change has taken place. But no one around them will know this until they see this person doing the things they were too lazy to do before.

Surely you've heard the childhood saying; "Sticks and stones will break my bones, but names will never hurt me." Well this isn't entirely true. "The sticks and stones" part is, but the "names will never hurt me" part is totally up to the person who's being called a name. A negative name, that is. If the negative "names" are coming from a loved one or a revered authoritative figure, they can hurt very badly. Mostly because we're shocked that this person is talking to us this way. If we love someone we want him or her to love us back. And if we hold someone in high regard we want him or her to at least like us. But if you're self-confidence is high enough, not even negative words coming from such a loved or respected person can hurt you. That is, unless they're speaking the truth. You know what they say about the truth; "it hurts." Remember what I said about no one knowing you better than you?

Sometimes we as humans portray ourselves differently on the outside than we really are on the inside. For instance, the so-called "friend". You know the person that forever smiles in someone's face, but behind their back they hate their guts. If the negative truth about this persons' deceit were spoken to them by a loved one or an authoritative figure it would more than likely hurt. Simply because this person may look one way on the outside, but they know in their own heart that they really are deceitful. **No amount of self-confidence will overcome a lie without becoming a lie itself.** So be honest with you first and foremost.

You might think; "How can I be confident if I don't have any abilities?" That's a lie. If you happen to believe this about yourself you need to stop it right now. Everyone has the ability to do something. We live in a world full of human beings. Not super human beings. Everyone has strengths and everyone has weaknesses. **Everyone!** Picture in your mind someone you feel is the epitome of human existence. Is it a movie star, a big business person, or maybe even your mom? It could be anyone. It really doesn't matter who it is. If they're human then they're no better than you or I. Every one of us makes mistakes. We all need air to breathe, food to eat, and rest for our bodies. We all have blood flowing through our veins. And eventually every one of us is going to die. I don't care how good you look, how much fame, fortune, or power you have, you are still a mortal human being. There are no super humans on this planet. You need not genuflect to anyone just because they're rich or famous. In fact, you need not genuflect to anyone for any reason. Because **you control your feelings.** If you feel inferior to someone who has more money than you, has a different shade of skin than you, or is even a few inches taller than you, it doesn't matter what the reason is, the problem is not with them, it's with you. See. It's not because that person makes you feel inferior. It's because **you believe** that they're somehow superior to you, and **you choose** to feel inferior. **Each and every one of us needs to know that we're in control of our feelings.** If you'll practice being confident you won't have feelings of inferiority anymore. You'll have feelings of confidence. The same goes for envy and any other negative feelings you might have. If you'll spend time concentrating on your own confidence and your own goals you won't be wasting your valuable time worrying about what someone else is or isn't doing.

Envy is especially stupid to me. I mean, think about it. Most people are envious of people they know little or nothing about. And on top of that they're envious about something that neither they nor the person they're envious of has any control over. For instance, two people doing the same job and only one of them gets promoted. Well, envy could rear its ugly head if the unpromoted person lets it. They could spend hour upon hour hating this promoted person, calling them names, spreading rumors, whatever. But if they'd stop and think for a minute they'd realize that someone had to promote this person. They didn't promote themselves. So the promotion wasn't something that was being controlled by this promoted person.

Okay. What if this person was a brown noser and that's why they got promoted? So what? Being a brown noser is no guarantee of career success. Sure some people reward brown nosers for their genuflecting ways, but by the same token others don't because they have no respect for them or their genuflecting ways. So **don't waste your time** hating so and so because they got a new car and you didn't. Don't go around spreading lies about this person or that person because good things always seem to happen to them and not you. Spend your time trying to raise yourself to a higher level rather than trying to pull someone else down. Believe me, you'll get where you're trying to go a lot faster if you'll channel your energies toward solving your own problems instead of trying to create some for someone else.

Okay. Back to self-confidence. Let's say some important event is about to take place in your life. It doesn't matter what the event is. It only matters that it's something that's important to you. Something that you desperately want to turn out in your favor. It could be anything from a marriage proposal to a basketball game. But for the sake of this analogy we'll say it's a job interview. Let's say you don't get the job. Things don't go your way. You go home and right away a loved one calls you a failure because you didn't get the job. Well. If your self-confidence isn't high enough, this negative "name" could indeed be very painful. In fact, something like this could lead you down the road to a deep depression. Because after all, you did "fail" to get the job. This is where self-confidence would override this negative assessment and render it helpless against you. Because there is no "failure" in self-confidence. Sure you may fail to get the job. You may fail to win the game. You may even fail to pass the test. But by no means does this make you a failure. None of the human race is perfect. We all make mistakes. We all "fail" from time to time. You've heard the saying; "A winner never quits and a quitter never wins." The latter part of this phrase is the definition of what a true failure really is. A quitter is one who, of his or her own free will, refuses to try again. Whether it is because of frustration, pride, stubbornness, or fear. Whatever the reason may be, they absolutely refuse to try again. They'll stand there, sit there, or lie there, without trying again; from now until the day they die. A person with this attitude can never expect to win.

A winner, on the other hand, never quits. Because this person knows that as long as they're alive they have a chance at winning. They may go through door #1 and meet with some sort of failure. Well. To the person with the winning attitude, this is but a temporary setback. Because there's always doors #2 through infinity. He or she just simply regroups and tries another door. They may even decide to go through door #1 again, this time doing something a little different than before. The point being is that there are countless ways for you to reach your goal. We all have to experiment with what works for us - what road we decide to take. But be self-confident, because if you've had any experience in life at all you know that negativity comes with the territory. There are negative situations that may arise and try to make you think you'll never reach your goal. There are also negative people who will not only tell you you'll never reach your goal, they'll also try to keep you from ever reaching it. These two "would be" hindrances would like nothing more than to see you, not only fail, but completely give up and become a total failure. So think highly of yourself at all times and the low estimation that some people may have of you will be of no effect to you.

Be self-confident in all you do! It doesn't matter whether it is for reasons I've stated here or reasons of your own. Because

I'm sure once you've tried it, you'll agree that being self-confident is better than being self-doubting any day.

Think about it!

SELF-MOTIVATION

Does this sound familiar? You're at your job, and for eight hours you do this or you do that. You run here or you run there. You type this or you type that. Or whatever it is you do all day or night or afternoon long. Then once you get home you automatically transform from Mr. or Ms. "Do Everything" into Mr. or Ms. "Do Nothing". You won't cook. You won't clean. You won't even wash yesterday's dirty dishes. Why? "Because I'm too tired from work," you might say. Well. While this is a legitimate gripe, think about all the times that you were tired at work. Did that stop you from getting your job done? I'd doubt it. Somehow you found the inner strength to get through your workday. How? Because you had a motivating force (your boss) behind you making sure you got your work done.

If you're like a lot of people you probably don't like your job. But even if you do, it may be something else you'd rather be doing. For instance, let's say you're a mechanical engineer, but deep down inside you long to be a surgeon. Maybe you don't have a job and lack the marketable skills to get a decent or high paying job. Maybe you want to run your own business. Whatever the case may be, the simple fact is that it's going to take some amount of time and effort to get from point A to point B. No one spends time training and working as a mechanical

21

engineer, then one day puts down his or her calculator, picks up a scalpel, and immediately becomes a surgeon. It just doesn't happen that way. If you want to be a surgeon, you're going to have to spend some time training to become a surgeon. And since most of us don't have the money to quit one job while we train for another, we'll probably have to pursue our heart-felt goal in our spare time. Whether it is your break time or lunchtime at work, or your free time at home after work, is totally up to you. This means that Mr. or Ms. "Do Nothing" will have to become self motivated and changed into Mr. or Ms. "Do Something". This may or may not be an easy thing to do depending on how lazy you are. Now when I say lazy I don't mean it in an insulting way. I think we're all lazy at some time or another. We all want that "path of least resistance" sometimes. If we had a choice we'd probably take it all the time.

Have you ever been walking into a building and come upon a group of two or more doors with only one door held open? If you have, I'm sure you've noticed that most people will head straight for the open door no matter what. It could be a line of people coming the other way, and some people will stand and wait to go through the open door rather than manually pushing or pulling open one of the closed doors. The same goes for automatically opened doors. Most people will wait to go through this door rather than take a second to open the manual door. The remote control is a big "path of least resistance" item. In this day and age almost every electronic gadget has a remote. Have you ever lost your television remote and found yourself walking right past the TV in search of it, without ever turning the TV on? Somehow turning the TV on manually has become a difficult task.

We want to cook faster, clean faster, travel faster, and most of all, get rich faster. Almost everything has to be faster and easier. And although there is absolutely nothing wrong with having things faster and easier, some things don't always come that way. Success is a thing I believe everyone wants. It doesn't matter whether it's financial, athletic, academic, or any other form of success. We all want to be successful at something. But success doesn't always come overnight. This is not to say that you won't be an overnight success. You may very well be. But what if you aren't? Will you lay down and quit, or will you stand up and fight? If you decide to stand up and fight you'll need to be motivated – Self-motivated.

The most important thing you need to realize in order to get yourself motivated is that **"Time waits for no one."** Look at your clock. Tick...Tock...Tick...Tock. It's ticking away this very minute. Every second of every day time marches on. You may think, as we all do at times, that we'll always have more time. But that's not true. Each of us has only so much time to live here on this earth. I once heard someone say; "The minute you're born you begin to die." This may sound morbid, but believe it or not, it's true. Death is not a subject that people like to discuss. Which I can't blame them because it's not a pleasing subject to talk about. None of us wants to die, so we push all thoughts of ever doing so into the back of our minds. Now I'm not saying that anyone should be sitting around pondering when and how he or she is going to die. I'm just saying that a lot of times we get a false sense that we'll be here forever. So we keep putting things off for another day, another month, another year. We sometimes take life for granted.

I'm almost sure you've seen some talk show or news report where some man, woman, or child, has just had a near death experience. They almost always say that now they have a new outlook on life. They appreciate it more. They **value their time** more. As well they should. Because time is more valuable than money. In fact, time is infinitely more valuable than money. You know why? Because you can gain and lose money again and again. But time you've got once and never again. It just keeps moving forward. You can't go back in time and you can't go forward in time. **The only time you've got is that second you're sitting on right now.** And as soon as you blink your eye it's gone. Well, you may say; "As soon as that one's gone there's another one taking its place." But the only thing is, you're not guaranteed that next second. You could be as alive as electricity when the clock ticks and dead as a doornail when it tocks. So don't waste your time being lazy or scared. Get up and do something constructive. Because as you know our time here on earth will one day end. And although money is a great thing to have, I'll bet if you had three million dollars and only three minutes to live, I know which one you'd rather have more of. You don't have to have a near death experience to have a new outlook on life. All you have to do is change your outlook on life. Did you hear that? **You have to change your outlook on life.** Nobody can do that for you. You must do it for yourself.

Now on the other hand you may think that some things take too long, therefore you won't bother to participate in them. For instance some people say; "After twelve years of school who wants to go another four, six, or eight years more." My answer to this is; "Don't let the time element dissuade you." Because believe it or not, four, six, or eight years will be here in exactly four, six, and eight years. Time is going to go on no matter what. You could spend that time going to school or you could spend that time hanging out on the corner getting high. You can spend your time doing something constructive or you can spend your time doing something destructive. You can even waste your time and do absolutely nothing. Time doesn't care what you do with it. But listen carefully to the terminology; **"your time."** It's not my time, your mom's time, or your friends' time. **It's your time,** and you'll have to choose what you'll do with it. You can go to school for eight years and become a doctor, or you can sit on the sidewalk for eight years talking about becoming a doctor. The choice is entirely up to you. I don't think you would want to look back on your life fifty or sixty years from now and say; "I should of, could of, or would of." You need to start saying right now, wherever you may be, or whatever situation you may be in; **"I shall, I can, and I will."** And remember this; **"If you'll start at something and keep moving toward that something eventually you'll reach that something."**

As I've said before; "No one can make you believe anything but you." and in addition; **"No one can make you do anything but you."** I know that we say and we hear all the time; "He made me do this, or she made me do that." But in order for anyone to "make" you do something they would have to literally take you over. For example, let's say you were walking down the street when suddenly someone approached you, pulled a gun, and demanded all your money. You, in compliance, gave them all your money. This is a case where most people would say; "They made me give them all my money." But that's not exactly true. They "asked" for all your money. They may have asked in a very harsh manner and placed you under extreme duress by pulling a gun, but they still didn't "make" you give them all your money. The point being is; you had a choice. You could've also said; "No." I wouldn't recommend you do this if you ever get into this situation, which I hope you never do, because it might get you shot. I'm merely saying, through the use of an extreme case, that the choice is there. In order for anyone to "make" you do anything they would have to take over your entire being, much like someone manipulates a hand held toy action figure, or maneuvers a subject in a video game. In almost any situation that you may face you'll have at the very least, two choices. The other choices may not be good ones, but they're still there. No one can "make" you do anything.

Too many times we make excuses for failure. Excuses like; "I don't have any time." or, "I can't learn math." or, "I don't have any money." The list could go on and on. And I'm not saying that any excuse is a good or bad excuse. I'm just saying it's an excuse. **There are only two things in this life that can keep you from achieving your goal: you and death.** Finding time is sometimes hard, but it's not impossible. Understanding math is sometimes hard, but it's not impossible. Making money is sometimes hard, but it's not impossible.

Hardships and obstacles in this life are not reserved for you and you alone. Although when you're faced with one it may seem this way. But believe me, there is someone somewhere who has made it through the same hard times that you're facing right now. And if they made it, so can you. This may not sound like much, but it's true. If you don't believe so, ask your friends, your parents, or your teachers to tell you some of the tough times they've faced in their lives. Read some successful persons autobiography. I'm sure that you'll find that we've all weathered some storms in our lives. And I'm also sure that some of these "storms" will sound very familiar, because you've gone through almost the exact same thing. Remember that you are surrounded by human beings. Not one of us is mistake proof, or armor plated. We all suffer our losses from time to time. We all have weaknesses, but we also all have strengths. So **don't make excuses for failure. Make excuses for success.** Excuses like; "I deserve to be happy." "Success is not discriminatory, It'll gladly be mine if I'll take it." or "The world needs someone as generous, compassionate, and kind as I."

You have to motivate yourself into seeing a brighter tomorrow, instead of wallowing in self-pity and depression because of what happened today. I'm not saying that this is an easy thing to do. But I am saying it's not an impossibility. You'll have to force yourself to see beyond the problems. Did you know that the sun always shines? Even when it's raining cats and dogs, hailing golf balls, or even snowing in sheets. The sun shines on. You may not be able to see that sunshine, but that doesn't mean its not there. It is, high above all those dark storm clouds. Too many times we focus on the storm and forget all about the sunshine above it. **We forget that storms never last forever.** We need to focus on our goal (our success) and not the temporary storms that may set us back a little. When we're hit with one of life's troubles, it's easy to fall down into a depression, cry and wonder; "Why me?" Remember what I said about the "path of least resistance?" Don't take the easy road unless it will benefit you. Depression is not a benefit. Listen to the terminology: depression; a hole. Don't dig a hole for you to lie down in and cry. The "why me" attitude is a waste of time. Fifteen minutes of depression is fifteen minutes of wasted time. Time that you'll never get back. When and if you're hit with one of life's troubles, don't think; "Why?" Instead think; "How?" How can I overcome this obstacle and prevent it from happening again.

Surely you've heard the expression, "If you want something done right, do it yourself." You know why this expression is true? Because you know better than anyone else on the face of this earth how you want something done. Of course we can't do everything, so we have to depend on others to do some things for us. But who better to get our lives together than us. And I don't know whether you realize this or not, but you could have the worlds' best motivational speaker talk to you everyday for the rest of your life, and if you don't want to get up off your butt and do something, you never will. **It is ALL up to U!**

Motivate yourself out of the weak and into the strong. Tell yourself that you are going to make it. Make yourself believe that you have the power to succeed. Just make sure the goals you pursue are truly your goals. They can't be your mom's, your dad's, your husband's, or your wife's goals for you. Because if your loved one wants you to be, let's say a doctor, and you really want to be a police officer, chances are you'll be miserable if you obey their wishes and become a doctor. Even though this is a good profession, it wouldn't fulfill you if you didn't want to be one. So make sure that you know - that you know - that you know - that you know - what it is that you really want to do. Don't insist on becoming something or doing something a certain way just because your best friend or next door neighbor became that or did it that way and it worked out really well for them. Do it because it's what you want to do. Because what worked for your best friend or your next door neighbor may not work for you. The what, when, where, why, and, how to reaching your goal is totally up to you. You may not have the foggiest idea of what it is you want to succeed in. But that doesn't mean you can't start preparing yourself with an attitude of attack. Then once you know what your goal is, you can tear right into achieving it. And all the naysayers and doubting Thomas's will have no effect on you, because you'll be motivated – Self-Motivated.

Think about it!

WHY WORRY?

Worry. Here's something that we've all done from time to time. In fact, you may be worried about something this very minute. But what is worry, and do we really need it?

The dictionary defines worry as mental disturbance due to care and anxiety; trouble; vexation; or torment. Looking at this definition, is this something that you really need? Of course not. Yet each and every one of us worries about something at some time or another. We worry about money. Usually the lack of it. We worry about our loved ones. We worry about our pets. We even worry about the weather. Anything that is cared about, you name it, and somebody somewhere has worried about it.

You might think it's perfectly natural to worry. Or you may think that you can't help but worry about some things. Well. I'm here to tell you that neither of these is true. You see, worry, plain and simple is nothing more than a form of fear. And believe it or not, you have a choice in whether you fear or not. You've heard the famous quote; "There's nothing to fear but fear itself." Well. Let's rephrase that and say; "There's nothing to be afraid of except being afraid itself." Or more simply put; "Be afraid to be afraid." This all may sound a little confusing, but all it's saying is don't be scared, don't be afraid, and don't fear.

Whenever you've had a problem, has worrying ever solved it? I doubt it. You don't ever get hit with some problem in life and say; "Oh, let me go worry about this and it'll go right away." No. It'll never happen. You may worry until your hair turns gray, but that won't do a thing towards solving your problem. Worrying about something, or fearing it, only puts undue stress and strain on your mind and body. This, in turn, could lead to other mental or physical ailments. So why do we worry? We worry because we feel helpless against the problem. We also fear the failure and subsequent pain that will most assuredly follow that problem. But if you'll stop and think a moment, worrying serves absolutely no purpose other than to harm you.

Let's say someone was in the jungle, armed with a high powered rifle. Suddenly, off in the distance, they see a snarling growling lion come charging toward them. The sight of this menacing beast headed for them, along with the thoughts of what it's going to do to them once it gets there, fills them with so much fear that they take their gun and kill themselves before the lion can.

In this little analogy, this someone represents you, me, or anybody else. The jungle represents our surroundings. The high powered rifle represents our talents and abilities. The lion, of course, represents the problems in our lives. Notice in the analogy, this person had the potential (high-powered rifle) to solve the problem (lion). They just didn't use it. They became so worried, or full of fear, that they forgot all about their own strengths and concentrated on the lions' strengths. Therefore causing them to harm themselves instead of the lion. This is what worrying does. It harms you while doing absolutely nothing towards solving the problem.

Now, don't get me wrong. When I say; "Don't worry." I don't mean for you to be carefree or care-less, as if there are no such things as problems. No. That's not what I'm saying at all. See? To care, or be concerned, is totally different than worrying. Concern, according to the dictionary, is defined as; "sincere interest." If a growling lion were charging towards you, of course you'd have a sincere interest in that. Or at least you should. The main and most important difference between worrying and being concerned is; "focus." When you worry, your focus is primarily on the problem and it's ability to overcome you.

For example, in the analogy, the person saw the lion coming from a distance, which, by the way, represents some amount of time. Because, believe it or not, it takes time to worry. If the lion had jumped on them unexpectedly, they would have been shocked, not worried. Okay. Getting back to "focus." The focus of the person in the analogy was clearly on the ferocious charging lion (the problem) and its' ability to harm them. Had

34

they been concerned, they would have acknowledged the problem of the charging lion, but instead of worrying about what the lion was going to do to them, they would have focused on their own strength (the rifle), and taken steps to halt the problem. There's your difference. **Worrying** focuses on the problem, producing nothing but a nervous breakdown or an ulcer or two. **Concern,** on the other hand, acknowledges the problem, but instead of focusing on it, turns and focuses on a solution instead.

Okay. Let's say the concerned person uses their rifle (talents and abilities) and the lion (problem) keeps coming. What do they do now? They fight! That's what. In life, as you well know, there are problems. Some big. Some small. We all encounter problems in our lives. It doesn't matter how good you look, how sweet you smell, or how much money you have. Some-thing, some-where, at some time, is going to present a problem to you. The key to beating worry when a problem does arise is in your decision to fight or not. And once you've made the decision to fight you must also decide to fight until you win. See? In the analogy, that person gave up before the lion (problem) ever got there. Which is how it is with a lot of people. They'll see a problem coming off in the distance, and instead of preparing to fight that problem, or stop it before it ever gets there, they give up. Then they worry and worry until they end up harming themselves instead of the problem. And still, the problem comes and overtakes them.

The problem doesn't care whether you fight or not. It only exists as a problem. And it will continue to be a problem, your problem, until you find some way of solving it. You need to motivate yourself to get up and take the necessary steps to solve that problem, whatever it may be.

Don't let fear keep you from taking a stand in life. Don't let it keep you from at least attempting to reach your goal. Like I said before; "Nobody knows you better than you." and ultimately "the choice is yours." You know what fears you have. So it's up to you to confront and overcome them. Don't sit around worrying. Fear is at the root of all worry. And besides that, worry has never solved anybody's problem.

Something else that may help to end the worry syndrome is putting the problem in a new light. Looking at it from a new perspective. For instance, let's say for some reason or another you can't make your car payments and the bank repossesses it. For most people this would be a harrowing experience. An experience in which you could worry and worry until you give up hope and slip into a depression. Because some of us use our cars so much it would be like having a life line cut. What you should do is put it in a different light and say something like; "I may have lost my car, but I still have my good health." This may sound a bit fruitless in dealing with something like the loss of a car. But if you stop and think about it a minute, that car, no matter what kind it is, could never compare to having good health. And besides that, if you're terribly sick and in pain, you're not thinking about and probably couldn't drive a car anyway. So anytime a problem hits, put it in a new light. It'll help keep you out of a depression. **Because things could always be worse.** On the other hand, you might say; **"Things could always be better."** Well, yes. But they won't be if you worry yourself into a depression. You certainly won't be thinking about solving your problem. You'll be worrying about; "Why has this happened to me?" or "What will people think of me?" The "why" part is worth knowing only for the purpose of preventing this problem from occurring again. But don't dwell on it, because the simple fact is that it has happened. So forget the self-pity and move on. As far as what people will say or think, it doesn't matter. As you probably already know, people will find something to say about you anyway. Sometimes they'll say good things. Sometimes they'll say bad things. None of it really matters.

The only opinion that ought to matter to you in this world, in this life, is yours. Because ultimately you are the one who has to live with the decisions you make. I'm not saying that your decisions won't effect other people, or that you should reject all other opinions. What I'm saying is; when you hear different viewpoints from other sources, you should digest and analyze these first. But when the final decision is made, it should be one that agrees with your heart. This, in fact, may agree totally with some of the other opinions. But no matter what the outcome, good or bad, you'll know that you've made the best possible choice for you.

Let's say you were unemployed. This, of course, is a big problem for a lot of people. You could sit around and worry and worry about the "why" and "why not" of your current unemployment. You could also sit around and, in an effort to escape the pain of worry, numb your mind with drugs or alcohol. Or you could get up and find some other means of employment. Whether it is company employment or self-employment is totally up to you. This last choice is the most difficult. That's why a lot of people decide upon the first two. Remember, we as human beings almost always desire the "path of least resistance." It's easy to sit around and worry. It's also easy to sit around and get stoned out of your mind. It's not so easy to stand up and deal with the rejection you may face during the course of looking for some new means of employment. This assumed rejection, I believe, is what keeps a lot of people from trying. Again worry is the culprit. They have a fear of being told "no", so they worry about this until it keeps them from even trying in the first place. This is a big mistake.

Don't pre-judge the outcome (at least not in a negative way). The only mind you can read is your own. And I'll bet you've even forgotten what was on it from time to time. For example, one minute you have something to tell someone, but the very next minute, when you see this person, you can't remember what it was you had to say. What happened to this information? Did it go to the "tip of your tongue?" So you see? We sometimes have a hard enough time remembering what we were thinking, without trying to second guess what someone else is. Besides, how many times have you thought the answer to your request would be "no", and it turned out to be "yes"? Not one of us can read minds and not one of us knows the future. You ought to at least try.

So what if you try and the answer is "no." Then what? In this situation you need to take this negative and turn it into a positive. I mean, you have to remember you're surrounded by imperfect humans. Humans that are bombarded with so much negative information (news, gossip, tabloids, etc.) that they sometimes lean this way. In fact, I'll bet if you tell ten people you know (friends, family, co-workers, etc.) that you're about to take on some risky endeavor like a complete career change, or investing your savings in a small business, the majority of them will tell you why you shouldn't. Probably with a doom and gloom story about what happened to them or someone they know. It's this negativity that makes them sometimes unable to recognize a diamond in the rough. So don't look at rejection as your loss, look at it as the rejecting party's loss. They're the ones who blew a chance to work with someone as generous, talented, and dedicated as you.

As I've said before, in order to eliminate worry you must decide to fight until you win. You have to take a "come hell or high water" attitude. This will help you forget about the negative and concentrate, or focus, on the positive. For example, I once heard a martial arts expert say; "Whenever he got into a fight he'd throw his life away." In other words, he was in this fight to the death if necessary. And he wasn't afraid to die. This eliminated any and all fears of being hit or hurt, and allowed him to focus on nothing but winning. If you think about it, it's the fear of death that's at the root of all fears. Why are people afraid of heights? Because they think they'll plummet to their death. Why are people afraid of bodies of water? Because they think they'll drown. Why are people afraid of enclosed spaces? Because they think they'll suffocate. All of these and many many more fall into the "might" category. That's what fear does. It causes you to "might" yourself into the wrong action or no action at all. You'll think this bad thing might happen or that bad thing might happen. But almost anything "might" happen. I mean, I could say; "King Kong might live on an island in the South Pacific." or "Dinosaurs might not be extinct." or "Aliens from Mars might be franchising burger joints throughout the United States and Canada." You see, "might" can go anywhere and everywhere your imagination will let it go. Remember this, **"The only difference between a hero and a coward is their decision."**

You can choose to be courageous and continue on your quest for your goal, or you can choose to fear and let negative speculation rob you of your focus and consequently, your goal. But if you'll eliminate fear, you won't have any problem focusing on your goal. And conversely, if you'll focus solely on your goal, you won't have any problem with fear. It's like when you're watching a really good movie. You won't hear the phone ring. You won't hear the dog bark. You won't even hear the person right next to you talking. Why? Because your mind is focused totally on that movie. It has your undivided attention. It is with this type of intense focus that you need to pursue your goals. So the next time someone asks you; "Aren't you afraid something will go wrong?" you can look them straight in the eye and say; "Why Worry?"

Think about it!

41

PRACTICE! PRACTICE! PRACTICE!

Practice. It's defined in the dictionary as; "Systematic exercise for instruction." or, "A custom or habit of doing something." Think about that. **Anything that you've ever done and gotten better at, you've had to practice.** It's like the cliche' says; "Practice makes perfect."

When we think about practice we normally think about sports or schoolwork. But if it's something to be done, whether physically, mentally, or spiritually, it can be practiced. Even something as routine as walking needs practice. If you were to lie in bed for some long period of time, say a year, without ever getting up, you'd have to be taught how to walk again.

Practice is basically repetition. You can repeat and repeat something until it becomes second nature to you. Think about all the different things in your life that once seemed impossible, but are now done with no difficulty at all. Your job, for instance. When you first started your job you were probably a little nervous about making mistakes or catching on quick enough. It was probably a little difficult too. But after being there day in and day out, getting all that practice, it no doubt became easier. Because **the more you look at something, do something, or study something, the more you'll understand that something.** Take for instance the cockpit of a typical commercial airliner.

Inside, there are enough buttons, knobs, and dials to intimidate any novice. But to the pilot and his or her crew, they present no mystery at all. Why? Practice. None of them just jumped in an airplane one day and soared into the wild blue yonder. No. It took time, practice time, to learn how to fly that plane. I can remember as a small child I thought that tying my shoes was the single most difficult procedure in the world. I couldn't understand how grown-ups had mastered such a complex set of maneuvers. All the crossing, looping, and pulling, boggled my mind. But after some practice, I was soon tying with as much confidence and precision as any grown-up. The point being is that; **"Anything that seems too difficult at first is soon made easy with practice."** I'm sure that you can think of many different things in your life that when you first encountered them seemed nearly impossible, but now are quite trivial. And furthermore, think about this; **"Everything is complicated until you understand it."**

Did you know that everything we know right now, we've learned? From the time we were born, up to this very minute. We've learned how to talk. We've learned how to walk. We've learned how to cross the street. We've learned good habits. We've also learned bad habits. How do we learn things? By practice (repetition). We do some "thing" over and over until we become familiar with it. We "learn" it. And anything that was learned can be "unlearned", if you will. Besides that, how do you think a habit becomes a habit? By practice, of course. No one becomes an alcoholic the first time they try alcohol. No one becomes a chain smoker the first time they try cigarettes. They practice drinking and smoking until it becomes second nature to them. I've heard people say that they continue to smoke, not because of the nicotine cravings, but because of the mere act of smoking. They've practiced this act so much that they wouldn't know what to do with their hands if they weren't holding a cigarette every so often.

Practice is the key to understanding something and getting better at it. You can practice almost anything. Even things like; self-confidence, eliminating fear, and having faith. You can practice things you're not even aware you're practicing. For instance, you hear a certain song on the radio every hour on the hour. Without consciously memorizing the words to that song, this constant repetition (or practice) will put them in your head anyway. And before long, you'll be able to repeat those lyrics verbatim. This principle holds true with all of our physical senses. You can taste, touch, smell, see, or hear some-thing so much, that without ever consciously trying to memorize that thing, you'll do it anyway. Advertisers know this. Although they primarily rely on your ability to see and hear. (These two senses don't require you to be close to the product.) This is why they use television and radio commercials with jazzy jingles and catchy phrases. They know the more you see and/or hear an ad, the better chance they have of getting you to buy their product. So what is all this seeing and hearing? It's practice, that's what.

Whatever it is, if you'll practice it, you'll get better at it. Why? Because practice (repetition) breeds familiarity. When you become familiar with something, you get to know it. And the known is always easier than the unknown is. Since we sometimes have a fear of the unknown, we often hold on to what we're familiar with, good or bad. How many times have you heard of someone staying in an abusive relationship? Why? Because as bad as this relationship may be, it's still something that's familiar to them. They don't want to let go of this clearly bad thing for fear that they'll run into something even worse. We do this with everything from jobs to hairstyles.

In order to stop practicing bad habits you have to start practicing good ones. In other words, **on the flip side of every bad habit is a good one.** The opposite of smoking is not smoking. The opposite of eating junk food is eating healthy food. The opposite of being lazy is being motivated. I know this all sounds simple, and at its most basic level it is. But we as humans don't always like to let go of the familiar, the things that we've become "used to." To practice things like; patience, self-confidence, eliminating worry, or any other intangible thing, mentioned in this book or otherwise, you'll first have to start talking to yourself. Whether it is out loud or in your head is totally up to you. I understand that this may sound a little strange to some people, but we talk to ourselves all the time. For instance, say you're walking down the street by yourself and you see an attractive person walk by. You'll say; "She's beautiful." or "He's handsome." Whether you say it out loud or in your head you're still talking to yourself. What about the time you misplaced your keys? I think we've all done this at one time or another. What do we ask ourselves; "Where did I put those keys?" See? It's not uncommon at all to talk to yourself. So if you're going to practice patience, you'll first have to tell yourself to be patient. (I will be patient.) You'll have to quit being anxious and make yourself wait a little while longer. This is much needed advice when you're in a hurry. Because, as you may already know, the whole world slows down when you're in a rush. You also make more mistakes when you're rushing. So whenever an opportunity arises for you to be anxious or in a rush, reject it. Then calm yourself and take comfort in the fact that it's almost always; "Better late than never."

What if you were a chronic procrastinator? You waited until the last minute to do everything from *your* taxes to washing the dishes. Again, you'll first have to tell yourself that this behavior *will* change. **Because, with time, you can change any**

behavior that you really want to change. Remember that there isn't anyone controlling *your* behavior via a joystick or control pad like some character in a video game. At every opportunity to procrastinate, turn it down. It's that simple. **YOU DO HAVE A CHOICE!** Make up *your* mind to force laziness out of your being. Practice "doing" until it becomes your natural instinct and that "waiting to do" *will* become a faint memory. Practice *will* work on anything that you put it to work on. That includes *your* temper, *your* shyness, *your* fear, and anything else that belongs to you. Yes. It, whatever "it" may be, belongs to you. Because when you practice "it", you get to know "it", and "it" becomes *yours*. Those are *your* basketball skills. That's *your* self-confidence. That's *your* drive and determination.

Notice in the last paragraph that I've italicized the words "your" and "will". This is because it is ***your will*** that will be the deciding factor in whether or not you practice something. I mean, it's easy to practice some sport if you love that sport. But what if you need a higher grade point average in order to play that sport? Now you have to practice something that you may not love so much. And it takes a strong will to practice things that may not be so interesting or enjoyable.

So if you need to get better at something, whatever that something may be, remember; **"Practice! Practice! Practice!"**

Think about it!

FAITH BREEDS PATIENCE AND PERSEVERANCE

Faith, Patience, and Perseverance go hand in hand on to success. I call them the "triumphant triplets." They are closely related and depend on one another to succeed. **Although faith is the key,** it opens the door to patience and perseverance. **You will not persevere without patience, and you will not have patience without faith.** This is simply because most successes in our lives don't happen immediately, or "overnight", as they say. It would be great if they did, but the fact is, most times they don't.

To have **faith** is to trust in something to the point that you'll act on that something. If you don't trust in some "thing", it is impossible to have faith in that thing. **Patience** is the ability to remain on an even keel. When you're patient you're not too high (anxious), and you're not too low (depressed), you're steady on course. **Perseverance** is a commitment to stay on course no matter what obstacles get in your way. Come "hell or high water" as the saying goes.

When you believe something so much that you know it in your heart and soul, it's impossible for anyone but you to change that belief. Take your name for instance. Let's say your name is Terry and you're 25 years old. Well Terry. What if I told you your name isn't really Terry, it's Dale? You'd tell me I was mistaken. And what if I told you again that your name is really Dale? Again, you'd tell me I was mistaken. You'd tell me your name is Terry. I could tell you a hundred times that your name is Dale and each time (if you stuck around that long) you'd tell me I was mistaken. Why? Because throughout you're 25 years of living you've been called Terry. And some time during that constant repetition of being referred to as Terry (Remember what I said about practicing things you're not aware of.), you believed, then came to know, that this is your name. And neither me nor anyone else would be able to convince you otherwise.

Now take a look at something else. You were hearing your name being called from two different places. First you were hearing it called from the outside by your parents, guardians, siblings, or friends. Then you believed, and you started hearing it called from the inside of you, coming from your own mouth. You started telling people, or "acting" like, your name is Terry. This, **hearing it from the inside, is what made you come to know** your name. Remember: "You'll believe you before you'll believe anyone else." and "You'll only act on what you believe." If I tell you your name is Dale and you tell you your name is Terry, which name are you going to respond (or act) to?

In order to obtain strong faith in something you're going to have to start hearing that something come from inside you. What I mean is; you're going to have to start concentrating on, and talking to yourself about that thing. It may be a little difficult at first, but eventually, as you practice "saying" whatever it is you want to have faith in, you'll start to see a clearer picture in your mind. The clearer this picture becomes, the stronger your faith will be.

Your mind is the deciding factor in whether you succeed or not. This is where all the information that you receive gets processed. Some of that information is negative and some of it is positive. But still it's up to you what information you keep in your mind and what information you discard. In other words, as I've said before, it's up to you what you believe. **If you want to have faith in something you're going to have to bombard yourself with positive information about that something.** You're going to have to speak up and tell yourself and all the negative forces around you that you will succeed. That may sound strange. But think about it. Doesn't that sound better than hearing, believing, and repeating all the negative reports? The reports that say you're not smart enough, strong enough, or pretty enough. The reports that say you'll never amount to anything. The reports that say the rich get richer and the poor get poorer.

If you'll continue to say good things about your success, you'll start to believe those good things. Then, once you fully believe, you'll start to act like those things are already true. You know why? Because to you they are. You can see them so clear in your mind that you can almost touch them. They might not be in your lap yet, but you know they will be soon. This is faith.

Furthermore, think about whatever "it" is you're believing for. Is it good health? Is it a good job? Is it a new home? Is it a large sum of money? Whatever it is, remember this; **"Anything that you'd ever need faith for is well within your reach."** I'll repeat that. Any "thing" that you'd ever need faith for is well within your reach. You know why? Because you can't have faith in something that doesn't exist, either in your world or the world around you. For example, what if I said; "I'd like to have a new car." Right away my mind has something identifiable to base my faith on: the car. I know what a car is; therefore I can have faith in obtaining one. The same is true for good health, a good job, a new home, a large sum of money, or anything else that you can identify. But what if I said; "I'd like to have a zozgogma." "A what?" you might say. See? I couldn't believe or have faith in getting a zozgogma simply because I don't know what a zozgogma is. I just made it up.

But on the other hand, what if I had an idea for this radical new invention that I chose to call a zozgogma? Well, now I can have faith in a zozgogma. Why? Because now I have a mental image of what a zozgogma is. I can identify it. The whole world may not know what it is, but I do, because I have that mental image. To me it exists. I can see it in my mind. Now I must take that mental image and produce a physical image so that the rest of the world can see and identify it. This is not only true of physical (or seen) things, but it's also true of unseen things. Things like self-confidence, courage, and patience. If you'll speak about yourself being confident, courageous, patient, and whatever else you'd like to be, you'll soon get a mental picture of yourself being these things. Then you'll start acting like these things are true. And guess what? They will be.

Faith is the key. It is an action word. If you have faith in something, you're either **moving toward** that something or **moving away** from that something. But you are moving. It is not just enough to believe. Believing is where you start. Faith will get you where you want to be. For example, someone watches a sporting event and says to themselves; "I can do that just as well, or better, than any of those players." The very next day this person finds out that the team is having tryouts. They decide not to go. This person may have believed that they had the ability to make the team, but they did not have faith in that ability. You can believe that physical exercise will make you stronger and healthier, but until you pick up the weights, or do the aerobics, you haven't expressed any faith. You will not be patient, you will not persevere, and you will not move, without first having faith.

Let's say you live in a relatively small city. You live at the north end of that city and your mom lives five miles away at the south end. One night you're talking on the phone when your mom suddenly says; "Get down here. Now." and the phone hangs up. You try to call back, to get more information, but now her line is busy. Immediately you head for your car. But once inside, you find it won't start. You run back in the house and try calling friends, none of which answers because it's too late in the evening. With no public transportation available, you decide to run the five miles.

During the first mile you get chased by a pack of stray dogs. During the second mile you trip and fall, tearing a big hole in the knee of your hundred dollar slacks. During the third mile your legs start to cramp. During the fourth mile it starts pouring down rain. Finally you reach your moms' house, exhausted, wet, and confused, only to find out she wasn't talking to you at all. Her beloved cat, Fluffy, had jumped from her lap to the top of the grandfather clock she was sitting next to. She was merely calling her back down. Only when she motioned for Fluffy to move, the phone cord was yanked out of the wall. And when she tried to call you back, she got no answer.

What made you move (or act)? Faith. What made you patient enough to run five miles in the middle of the night? Faith. What made you persevere through all of the obstacles and mishaps that befell you? Faith. And where was that faith coming from? Inside you of course. It was the faith in your mothers' words; "Get down here. Now." that made you act. It was these same words that entered your mind. Then you chose to believe them. And once you fully believed them you no doubt repeated them, in your head or out loud, during your journey. But notice something here; those words first came from the outside of you. (You heard them.) Once inside you, you made the choice to believe them. (You decided to believe what you'd heard.) Once you fully believed them you acted on them. (You moved because of faith.) And while you were acting, those words came from inside you. (You spoke the words, silently or aloud, that you had faith in.)

Don't get discouraged because of the way things are today. You have to look forward and expect the best. Let's say you're fighting the "battle of the bulge." You can't expect for thirty or forty pounds to drop off of you in a day or two. You'd probably become very sick if it did. You must remember that certain things take time. Losing weight is one of those things. You've heard the saying; "Rome wasn't built in a day." Well. It wasn't. And you won't go from an overweight individual to Mr. or Ms. Universe in a day either. Also, **don't base your success on the success of someone else.** For instance, what if you and a friend were doing the same exercises and eating the same foods, but they were losing ten pounds per month while you were losing only five? This might cause you some stress, depression, or maybe even envy. Though it shouldn't. Because whether you know it or not, you can't do a thing in this world about the interior make up of someone else. You may have to do twice the exercise and eat half the food to lose ten pounds per month. In other words, you'll have to **try harder**. This goes for everything from basketball to rocket science. The person next to you may exel at one thing or another. For them it comes easy. You, on the other hand, if you want to reach that persons level or beyond, will have to work two, maybe three times harder. This takes faith, strong faith. **You must believe, to the point of knowing that your goal is attainable.**

Picture yourself walking up the "down" escalator. Imagine that your goal is at the top. On this journey you'll have to work a little harder to get to your goal because you've got negative forces working against you all the time, trying to pull you down. But the harder you work, the faster you'll get there. And notice, if you stop or give up you'll go right back to where you started: the bottom. So hang in there, keep the faith, remain patient, and endeavor to persevere. Because with these three ingredients you've got the perfect recipe for success.

Think about it!

WHO NEEDS IT? (BEATING ADDICTIONS)

What is an addiction? An addiction is nothing more than a "needed" habit. I put "needed" in quotation marks because the "need" for a person's particular habit is usually all in that persons mind. It is this perceived "need" that drives people to do some pretty strange things when trying to satisfy their addiction. The "need" usually stems from some fear, false promise, or some wanted feeling of pleasure. For instance, people who've become addicted to vomiting after they eat (bulimia), usually have a fear that they'll get fat if they digest their food. People who constantly gamble keep believing the false promise that next time they're gonna strike it rich. And people who've become addicted to alcohol, among many other drugs, usually want that pleasurable feeling of being "high." They want to be "high" above all their fears, doubts, and problems. Now don't get me wrong here. I'm not talking about people who constantly behave a certain way because of some mental disorder. I'm talking about healthy people that have **let** themselves become addicted.

You can develop a habit, or an addiction, to almost anything. There are people addicted to drugs, food, and alcohol. But there are also people addicted to washing their hands, cleaning their homes, and grinding their teeth. There is no set list of things that one can or cannot become addicted to; there are just people and their seemingly uncontrollable desires to do some "thing."

Don't confuse an addiction with a habit. Habit is defined as; a settled tendency or practice, and/or a customary manner of action. There are plenty of habits that are not addictions. For instance; bathing, brushing your teeth, or styling your hair. **A habit becomes an addiction when you lose control of the frequency of the (act or thing)...**

Let's say you have a habit of taking a shower each morning before you start your day. In my opinion, this is a good habit. This becomes an addiction when you "need" to take a shower after even the smallest encounters with dirt; such as brushing against a dusty surface, or getting a pencil smudge on your hand.

...And when missing the (act or thing) causes you some great amount of stress.

Let's say you own a rabbit's foot. To some this would be considered a harmless novelty. But what if you lost this "lucky" charm and found yourself tearing up the house in search of it, because you absolutely can not make an important decision without it? If this were you, I'd say you were addicted to that severed rodent's appendage.

So how do we beat addictions? Well. First of all, as with anything that you're going to change about yourself, you're going to have to change the way you think. You'll have to look at things from a different perspective. For instance, have you ever wanted to be a slave? No? I didn't think so. But that's exactly what you are if you're addicted to some product or activity. Every time that "thing" calls, you come running, no matter what the circumstances. It becomes the master and you become the slave.

You need to realize that you are in control of your actions. Once you realize this, you'll have a much better chance at beating any addiction. See? No one makes a junkie constantly use drugs. No one makes an alcoholic constantly drink alcohol. No one makes a bulimic constantly throw up his or her food. No one makes a gambler take chance after chance. They do these things of their own free will. Yes. The temptation to give in to these addictions may be strong, but that's no excuse. The fear that one feels may be humongous. The pleasure that one gets may be oh so tantalizing. But it's still the conscious choice of the individual to continue their addictive behavior. Their "will" is still free. It may be extremely weak in some particular area, but it's still free. If it were not, then we'd have to say that this person is possessed by something that makes them continually repeat certain behavior. Which, in my opinion, is not true most of the time.

Temptation is only strong when you are weak. For instance, two people are seated opposite each other at a small round table. In the center of the table is a bottle of liquor. One of these individuals is an alcoholic. Both are asked not to drink any of the alcohol. For one person this request poses no problem at all. This person is strong in this area and temptation is very weak. But for the alcoholic, resisting a drink from the bottle is an intense struggle. One that he or she may very well lose. This person is extremely weak in this area and temptation is very strong. Notice that in both cases **the degree of temptation is always dependent upon and directly opposite the person's strength.** Temptation cannot be strong without you being weak, and it cannot be weak without you being strong. **The fifty billion-dollar question is; "Will you be weak or strong?" The choice is yours and yours alone.**

When you're in the middle of a temptation battle you need to concentrate on the end result, not the activity. What I mean is, think about the negative side of the addiction rather than the activity itself. For instance, when you're receiving the great temptation sales pitch. You're hearing the little voices tell you how great it felt before and how great it's going to feel now. They tell you you're definitely going to win this time. They entice you to try it just once more, or threaten you with what will happen if you don't. They'll give you reason after reason to give in. **You need to know that you are the deciding factor.** If you'll focus on the end result of the activity and look at the trouble it could cause, or may have already caused on previous occasions, you'll have a much better chance of defeating the addiction. Because, as you may already know, **that fear that is trying to push you, or that pleasure that is trying to pull you, is not worth the pain that may follow.** A.I.D.S. is not worth it. Financial ruin is not worth it. Prison is not worth it. Death is not worth it. No addiction is worth your health and well being. So stop selling yourself short and falling prey to that addiction.

In order to overcome a particular addiction you're going to have to transform yourself from a weak person, where this particular addiction is concerned, into a strong person, where this particular addiction is concerned. What I mean is, you're going to have to become bigger and stronger than the desire for that particular activity. And despite what anybody says, no amount of books (this one included), no amount of rehabs, and no amount of counseling, is going to cure you of that addiction if you don't really want to be cured. As I've said before; "We all have certain strengths and we all have certain weaknesses." It's these weaknesses that can lead us down the road to an addiction. So you'll have to take that weakness that's keeping you "hooked" and become strong in that area.

Let's say you were addicted to cigarettes and trying to quit. You need to answer the question; "Why?" Do you smoke because you think you look "cool" when doing so? Do you smoke because you like the feeling of warm smoke entering your lungs? Do you smoke because you're physically dependent upon nicotine? You need to find the reason or reasons you smoke, then make a quality decision to rid yourself of that addiction. Understand that, for many people, the eradication of an addiction is a very difficult thing to do. Simply because, if you fear something so much or desire something so greatly that it has caused you to participate in some activity so often that this activity has become second nature, once you decide to quit this activity, your mind and body will fight you tooth and nail. So whatever the addiction, get ready for a fight.

In the case of cigarettes, your body will more than likely crave the nicotine and your mind will try to convince you that you "need" a smoke. But do you really "need" that smoke? Will you keel over and die if you don't get that smoke? Is that smoke providing nourishment to your body, or is it slowly and silently eroding your health? If you're honest with yourself you know the answers to these questions are "no", "no", and, "slowly and silently eroding your health", respectively. Still. This approach will help some people and others it won't.

You may or may not care that you're inhaling nicotine (a poisonous alkaloid) into your body every time you smoke. You probably don't think about the long-term effects: whether or not it's hurting you, your loved ones, or your unborn child. All you want is your smoke. Lung cancer, emphysema, or any other "smoking related" disease always happens to someone else. It'll never happen to you. This attitude is pure selfishness. You need to look at how this addiction is affecting the people around you. You need to find something in your life that is more important than that addiction. It may be a loved one. It may be your health. Whatever the reason, you'll need to keep it on your mind as much as you possibly can. Because whenever the temptation comes you'll need this reason to anchor your thoughts, hold you steady, and keep you from succumbing to that addiction again.

Did you know that an inanimate object is influencing you? I don't care if it's a narcotic, an alcoholic drink, or a small cylindrical piece of paper stuffed with tobacco; they're all inanimate objects. That narcotic can't force itself into your body if you don't want it in your body. That alcoholic drink can't force itself down your throat if you don't want it down your throat. That cigarette can't light itself and jump into your mouth if you don't want it in your mouth. So stop being the slave to an inanimate object. **If you're addicted to narcotics, alcohol, or cigarettes, stand up and tell them that they no longer rule your life or influence your actions, you do.** Become the master of your body instead of the slave of some inanimate object.

Listen to this; "To be "high" is to be in-**toxic**-ated." Depending on the type of drug you take (nicotine and alcohol are drugs), you are ingesting enough toxins into your body to slow it down, speed it up, make you have hallucinations, or some combination of these things. And although ordinary cigarettes won't get you a D.U.I. charge, they are filled with toxins. Have you ever noticed that a lot of people smoke to relax or calm themselves? And what about D.U.I. (Driving Under the Influence)? Under the influence of what? Drugs, that's what.

Why on earth would you want to abandon your good sense to follow the influence of some toxic filled drug? For pleasure? There's no pleasure in feeling your heart beat so fast you think it's about to explode. There's no pleasure in feeling your heart beat so slow you think it's about to stop. There's no pleasure in hallucinating about demons, giant bugs, or dead people, coming to kill you. There's no pleasure in getting your face bashed in because, in your intoxicated state, you challenged someone to a fight that you probably couldn't have beaten had you been completely sober. There's no pleasure in coming down from your "high" only to find out you've just killed someone and will probably be spending a good portion, if not the rest, of your life in prison. There's no pleasure in having your back split open because the doctor has to remove your useless tar filled lung.

There's no pleasure in dying with a cirrhotic liver. Tell me, where is the pleasure in these things? There is none.

I'm not saying that any of these things have or will happen to you. But why take the chance? You need to look at the long-term effects that these drugs can have on you. I understand that you may have a friend or loved one that has used some drug or drugs most of their lives with no visible adverse effects from it. So what? First of all, you don't know how that prolonged use of drugs has affected that person on the inside. And secondly, you don't know what effect prolonged use will have on you. **Everything that you put into your body has some effect on your body.** The food you eat, the liquid you drink, the drug you take. If it goes into your body it has to affect your body in some way. Some things we ingest have very good effects. Others have very bad effects. While still others have hidden or false effects. They give the feeling of a good effect while slowly tearing away at your health and well being. It's these hidden or false effects that we so often become addicted to. They provide immediate gratification while slowly eating away, or weakening, our insides. Why take the chance?

Let me ask you this; "What if there were some new product on the market that would give you the most incredible feeling in the world for five full days? But at the end of the fifth day you were sure to die an excruciatingly painful death. What do you think the success rate of this product would be?" Terrible I'd say. You know why? Not just because of the painful death, but because of the "guarantee" of the painful death. Sure you'd have some very misguided people that would try it anyway, but not many. Because we as humans, though we abuse our bodies day in and day out, don't really want to die. And especially not a painful death. If everybody that was addicted to some "thing" knew, without a doubt, that that "thing" was going to kill them in the very near future, I think you'd see a lot of people kicking the habit "overnight." This tells me that most people remain addicted, not because they can't quit, but because they don't really want to quit.

If you use food or drugs to calm your nerves, you need to take a long hard look at what's causing your nerves to become so rattled in the first place. For instance, some people drink alcohol, smoke cigarettes, or use narcotics, to relieve the "stress of the job." If this is you, you need to find the cause of the stress. Is it fear of your boss and his constant threats? Is it fear of making a mistake and possibly getting fired? Is it fear of the rumor mill that almost always spits out some scandalous gossip with your name attached? It could be any reason. But as you can see, they're all based on fear. It is this fear you must address and overcome. Then you won't need any alcohol, cigarettes, or narcotics, to calm your nerves due to the "stress of the job." Because there won't be any fear to cause any stress.

As for those addictions related to an extreme fear, you'll have to, again, confront and overcome that fear. See? Fear is nothing more than faith in a bad thing. If I fear you, I have faith in your ability to harm me. If you're constantly participating in some activity that you'd like to stop, but seemingly can't because of fear of some grave consequence if you do, then you need to confront that fear. You need to muster up the courage to stand against that fear. Because just like temptation, fear is only strong when you are weak. **Fear cannot overtake you unless you let it.** Fear overcomes you because you drop all your mental defenses and let it rush in. You stop believing all the good things that can happen and start believing all the bad things that can happen. Aren't you tired of losing to that fear all the time? Every time it rears its ugly head, you cower into some corner of your mind and submit. Yes. **Fear is all in your mind.** You fear heights because you're hearing in your mind, and believing, that you might fall and kill yourself. You fear digesting your food because you're hearing in your mind, and believing, that if you do so you'll get fat and be perceived as ugly by society. Remember; "Only what you truly believe is going to affect your actions."

In order to defeat fear you need to change your mind, or in other words, start believing the positive (your success) instead of the negative (your failure). I'm not saying that this will be an easy thing to do. But by the same token, I'm not saying that it will be an extremely difficult thing to do either. As I've said before, "We all have strengths and weaknesses." Quickly changing your beliefs for your benefit may be a strength of yours. But for most people, I dare say, who've been believing something for some extended amount of time, they're not likely to change that belief overnight. So if this is you. You'll, more than likely, have to work at it. Remember; "Practice! Practice! Practice!"

Think about when you were a baby. You probably didn't have very many fears. Why? Because you didn't know about all the negative things of this world. So what caused you to fear certain things and not others? Was it some terrible accident? Was it horrible treatment or betrayal by someone you trusted? Was it the morbid news reports we hear sometimes three and four times a day? It doesn't matter what the reason or reasons may be. The point being is that **you were not born with that fear.** You allowed it into your thinking, and then into your belief system at one time or another in your life. Now, in order to discontinue that addictive behavior, you must overcome that fear. But how? As I've said before; "You must fight!" I don't know whether you know it or not, but you're in a fight for control of your life. And if you're addicted to some negative thing in your life right now, you're losing that fight. See? That addiction wants to control you by seducing you with pleasure or intimidating you with fear. It wants to keep you in bondage. So what are you going to do about it? Fight! That's what. **You must fight (mentally) to control your beliefs.** Because remember, you'll only act on what you believe. If you'll convince yourself (or believe) that you're bigger, stronger, tougher, and smarter than those negative thoughts (and you are), you won't have any problem defeating that fear. And once you defeat fear, you're back in control of your life. You won't "need" to throw up your food because you won't have any fear of getting, or being perceived as, fat. You won't "need" to wash your hands every few minutes because you won't have any fear of germs attacking your body. You won't "need" to get high to calm your nerves because there won't be any fear to cause your nerves to be rattled in the first place. You won't "need" to do anything you don't want to do because fear won't be able to bully you in to doing something you don't want to do.

So fight, fight, fight, and drive fear out of your mind. You ought to take on what I call a "cat in a corner" attitude. What do I mean by this? Think about an ordinary docile house cat. This animal will more than likely run the other way every time you threaten it. But if you back this same docile creature into a corner and threaten it, you'd better watch out. This cat now has a new attitude. Its fangs are exposed. Its back is hunched and its claws are ready to strike. This cat has one thing on it's mind; survival. And it doesn't mind fighting to stay alive. It will fight you and anything else that corners it, threatening to take its life. This is the attitude you need to take. If fear has you backed into a corner, threatening to take control of **your life**, you need to change your attitude and come out fighting.

The choices you make in your life are yours and yours alone. Let me ask you a question; "Do you really want to beat this addiction?" See? No one really knows the answer to this question but you. And even if you were to tell me your answer was "yes", I still wouldn't really know you'd meant it until you'd proven it, over time, through your actions. (We've all said things we didn't really mean.) Your actions reveal the truthfulness of your words. Because I can tell you a thousand times that I want to quit some detrimental behavior, but if I don't change my ways (or actions) to coincide with what I've said, then you know I've lied.

Remember this; **"As long as you tolerate some "bad" thing, you'll always have that "bad" thing."** If you're addicted to some "thing" or some "activity" that you'd like to stop, **change your mind.** Tell yourself; **"You can and will beat**

this thing." Then ask yourself; "Who "needs" it?" Your answer should be; "Definitely not you."

Think about it!

ME, MYSELF, AND I

I'm sure you've heard the expression; "Me, Myself and I." These of course referring to oneself as a trio. Though it's a very common cliche', I'd bet that the many people that use it have little or no idea that they're speaking a truth.

ME (BODY)

Me, is what you and I see when we look in the mirror. It is merely the physical, flesh and blood "house" that **Myself** and **I** live in. It could be black, white, fat, skinny, tall, short, or have any number of different characteristics. But all in all it's still only a container, or vessel, for your mind and your spirit.

It can be strengthened primarily through physical means. You almost always have to eat physical food and exercise your body in some physical manner; running, weight lifting, swimming, etc., in order to increase your physical strength.

MYSELF (MIND)

Myself, is referring to the mind. My mind, your mind, anybody's mind. It is the **bridge** between the physical (your tangible brain) and the spiritual (your intangible spirit). It is located in both. This is why we can learn things through our five physical senses, but we can also learn things through our spirit, or what we usually call intuition. Somehow we know something that didn't get into our heads through sight, touch, taste, feel, or hearing. It came from our spirit. Notice this also; we can learn both tangible things (printed words), and intangible things (spoken words).

Just as with the body, or the physical part of oneself, the mind can be strengthened as well. But instead of physical training, it's mostly strengthened through mental exercises like concentration, meditation, or memorization. The body is physical. The mind is mental. Two separate entities. Which brings us to...

I (SPIRIT)

I, the spirit, ones inner self. It looks just like you, only it's not physical and it's not mental, it's spiritual. This is the part of the human make-up that a lot of people have a problem with. They know they have a body and they know they have a mind, but they're not too sure about, or just flat out don't believe that they have a spirit. (Actually you are a spirit, who has a mind, and lives in a body.)

See? The word spirit is synonymous with the word ghost. And because a lot of people have been taught since childhood that there are no such things as ghosts, as adults they hold firm to the old adage; "I'll believe it when I see it." But think about this; there are plenty of things you can't see that you use everyday. Air, microwaves, and molecules, just to name a few. You can't see air but you breathe it every few seconds of every day of your life. You'd be dead soon without it. You can't see microwaves. But you can definitely see the effects they have on food. You can change a frozen piece of food into a boiling hot piece of food by penetrating it with invisible microwaves. And last but not least, you can't see the molecules that make up the water you drink, the air you breathe, the chair you sit in, or even this book you're reading. But they're there.

Think about numbers for a minute. Numbers are infinitely positive (or larger), and infinitely negative (or smaller). What if I took a ball and magically doubled it's size every second. Can you see how that ball would grow until it stretched across the universe? Take the same ball and magically decrease it's size by one half every second. Now can you see how that ball would soon be invisible, not only to the naked eye, but also to any and all human made magnifying devices? Why? Because no matter how small that ball gets, you can still divide it in half.

Everything visible to the naked eye is made up of smaller components that are not visible to the naked eye. Furthermore, think about this; "Everything seen was first unseen." Every seen thing started out as some unseen idea, whether in the mind of man (cars, toasters, paintings, etc.), or the mind of God (mankind, animals, planets, etc.). So you see; "I'll believe it when I see it." is not a very good rule to live by. Besides if you see it with your naked eye, chances are, you'd know it. You don't need to believe it. You know you're reading this book, you don't need to believe you're reading it.

While the body primarily needs physical exercise to be strengthened, and the mind primarily needs mental exercise, the spirit indeed needs spiritual exercise to be strengthened. The reason I say the mind and body "primarily" need mental and physical exercise to be strengthened is because the spirit can strengthen them both. And although a rare occurrence, there have been cases of people gaining superhuman strength, or uncanny mental ability when faced with some dire situation?

See? Our spirits are what keep us alive. Once it leaves, the body dies. This is why a person must be brain dead to be legally dead. Once the bridge is broken, the mind and spirit separate from the body and the body dies. Surely you've heard of someone dying from "natural causes." They didn't die from disease, and they didn't die from trauma, their mind and spirit simply separated from their body.

Think about it!

BELIEVE IT OR NOT (THE CHOICE IS YOURS)

Almost everything in this book is my opinion or view on one thing or another. An opinion or view that you may choose to accept or reject as you exercise your right to your opinion or view. What you are about to read now may delight you. It may scare you. It may even offend you. All I ask is that you read it with an objective mind. (**Think about it!**)

There are various tomes of various religions that claim to be spiritually oriented. But the only one I could recommend is the Holy Bible. It is my belief that the Bible is the word of God. It is spiritual, and it is truth. Gods' word is spiritual because He is a spirit. It is truth because, unlike us, He has the power to uphold (or bring to pass) anything and everything that He says. His word truly is His bond.

Wait a minute before you run for the hills, or toss this book into the fireplace or garbage. I just want to present to you a little common sense. I don't claim to have all the answers, but I'm trying to lead you to someone who does.

The existence of God, one true God, is a touchy subject for a lot of people. I know a lot of different people worship a lot of different gods, but the God I am referring to though, is the God of the Holy Bible. God the Father, the Son, and the Holy Spirit.

He is three manifestations, much like you are a spirit that has a mind and lives in a body. But unlike us, whose mind, body, and spirit are often at odds with each other, (How many times has your mind said "no" and your body said "yes"?), these three agree totally, all the time. This is what makes them "one." That's why Jesus can say, in the book of John, chapter 14, and verse 7; "If you've seen me, you've seen the father." God is the Father of our Lord and Savior Jesus the Christ (Anointed), creator of all things, and everything that I've written in this book, from beginning to end, was in some way based on my belief in God and His Word.

A lot of people believe those millions of years ago we started out as several elements. These elements, through chemical reactions, formed to make one-celled organisms. These organisms, through chance mutations, later evolved into animals, one of which was the ape. Then from these apes evolved mankind. My question to this "theory" is; "Where did the elements come from?" Who created them? Everything came from somewhere. If we evolved from apes millions, billions, or even trillions of years ago, why aren't there apes walking out of the jungle today looking to get a shave, a briefcase, and a three piece suit? Because today is the first day from a million years ago, a billion years ago, a trillion years ago, or infinite years ago. How come some apes evolved into men and other apes remained apes? Did they miss the evolutionary window? I guess mosquitoes evolved into birds, and salamanders evolved into horses? I guess you can see by now that the "Theory of Evolution" doesn't make much sense to me. I mean, how do you explain the thousands of different kinds of mammals, fish, insects, birds, worms, fungi, mollusks, reptiles, crustaceans, amphibians, and plant life too? How do you explain their reproductive organs? How do explain their innate sense to mate with their own kind? You don't see spiders trying to mate with snakes. Nor do you see birds trying to mate with bears.

How do you explain all the constants in this world? Things like electricity, gravity, or the elements. The laws that govern electricity are the same anywhere in this world. The law of gravity is the same anywhere in this world. The elements, from Actinium to Zirconium, are the same anywhere in this world. How do you get such constants unless they were deliberately created? You can't add a couple billion years and explain everything away with time. Time can't answer all these questions. There are many many questions that could arise from this "theory." Which leads me to believe that all of the many things of this world could not have possibly evolved from anything.

Now I know that there are people that seem to have an answer for everything when it comes to this "Theory of

Evolution." But listen to the terminology and it will tell you what it is. It's a guess. A "theory" is nothing more than a guess. It may be a highly educated one, but it's still a guess. Here's a question that you may or may not have heard before; "What came first, the chicken or the egg?" I'm here to tell you that the chicken came first. Do you know why? Because God made the chicken first. Then the chicken laid the eggs. God made the plants, the animals, and mankind too. Then all these different species reproduced and made more of their kind. If you don't believe this is true, let me ask you this; What did automobiles evolve from? Nothing. Correct? Why? Because mankind created them. So if mankind, in all his frailty, has the ability to create cars, and buses, and boats, and computers, and tools, and thousands of other things, why is it so hard to believe that God created the thousands of different mammals, and fish, and plants, and insects, and all the other wonderful life we have here on this planet?

Take a look at your money. Every piece of your American money has "In God We Trust" written on it. Why? Because this country was founded on God. This is the reason I believe it's so blessed. Now I didn't say it was a perfect country. Oh no. You and I both know this isn't the case. But have you ever noticed that people from all over the world want to come here? Not only to visit but also to live. They know or at least they believe that America is a blessed nation; a land of opportunity.

Okay. Take a look at your calendar. Now take a look at the day and date on your watch. What's today's date? It's somewhere between January and December, between the 1st and the 31st, nineteen hundred or two thousand whatever. You're not going to get on a plane in Philadelphia on May 1st, 1994, travel for fifteen hours, get off in Japan, and the date there is January 17th, 1834. No. It's not going to happen. You know why? Because the entire world keeps the same time (give or take a few hours because of time zones). So-called good countries keep the same time as so-called bad countries. People who do believe that Jesus is the Son of God keep the same time as people who don't believe He's the Son of God. The point I'm trying to make is; the very time we keep, not only in this country, but throughout the world, is based on the life of the Lord Jesus Christ; the Son of God. That, to me, is strong. I mean, very very very strong.

This man must have been everything that he said he was, and he must have done everything that he said he would. Surely you've heard of BC (Before Christ) and AD (Anno Domini - In the year of our Lord.). Some people say After Death, referring to the crucifixion of Jesus Christ. Think about that the next time you need to know what time it is.

81

Let's talk about names. There have been men and women throughout history that have done some very memorable things. Things so memorable that they'll be remembered for years to come. Names like Jesus...Cleopatra...Moses...Joan of Arc...Mary, the mother of Jesus...Columbus...Adolph Hitler...Albert Einstein...John F. Kennedy...Martin Luther King Jr...Malcolm X...Attila the Hun...Caesar...Napoleon Boneparte...George Washington...Nero...Michaelangelo... Socrates...Sir Isaac Newton...etc...Etc. Some lived long ago. Some lived not so long ago. Some have positive connotations with their names and some have negative connotations with their names. But with all due respect to these people, not one of them or any other largely famous person, whether good or bad, has had time, as we know it based on their life here on earth. None that is, except Jesus.

Okay. Here's some more about names. Think about the name God. You can't think of this name being anything other than superior. It doesn't matter what you apply it to. Once you apply it to something, that something is having superiority applied to it. You could say; "This horse is the god of all horses." Surely horses aren't gods, but right away you'd think there was something pretty special about that horse. Why? Because it's had the name "god" applied to it. The name is synonymous with superior, biggest, strongest, wisest, supernatural, or above natural limitations. You wouldn't call the baseball team with the worst record, the gods of the league. No. Why? Because they're below everyone else. You might call them some other choice names, but I'd doubt you'd call them gods.

How many times have you heard or even used the name God, or the name Jesus? A lot of times they're not used in their honor, but you hear them all the time anyway. Someone may get some good news and they'll say; "Thank God!" Sometimes when things don't go a certain way (our way) we may say; "God damn it!" (Which by the way, is useless request because God isn't looking to damn anything.) What about those pleasurable moments during lovemaking? What do you say; "Oh God!" or, "Oh God yes!" What about when someone disappoints someone else? The disappointed person often says; "Jesus Christ!" Even when someone sees something that shocks or awes them, they say; "God almighty or Christ almighty!" You don't hear people saying; "Thank Eve! Oh Ghandi!, or, Aristotle almighty!" No. Why? Because these people, though known in history, were not unlike you or I. They may be held in very high regard, but I'd doubt very seriously if anyone worships them as gods. And even if some do, I'd have to say that they've missed the mark. Because there is only one true God, one true Jesus the Christ (or anointed one of God), and one true Holy Spirit. There are many different ways in which the names of God and Jesus are used. I'm sure that at least one of my examples sounds familiar because they're used all the time. Not only in everyday conversation, but also in radio, television, and film. This is because God through His Son Jesus, and by the Holy Spirit, created mankind.

In the book of Genesis in the Bible, from chapter 2, verse 7, it says; "God formed the man from the dust of the ground and breathed into his nostrils the breath of life, and man became a living being." From this verse I'd like to call your attention to some things.

First; "God formed the man from the dust of the ground..." Did you know that a dead body will soon turn to dust, the substance from which it was made? It doesn't turn into an ameba, as some believe it evolved from. The Bible also says in that same book of Genesis, chapter 3, verse 19, in God speaking to Adam (the first man); "By the sweat of your brow you will eat your food until you return to the ground, since from it you were taken; for dust you are and to dust you will return."

Secondly, "God breathed into his nostrils the breath of life, and man became a living being." Okay. Notice here that even though God made the man from the dust of the ground, he still wasn't living until God breathed the breath of life into his nostrils. God breathed His Spirit into man and gave him life (man's spirit). From that moment on, mankind has known and will always know that there is a God. He or she may not choose to acknowledge God the Father, the Son, and the Holy Spirit, as Deity, but mankind will always have some other substitute for God. Whether it is he or herself, another human being, some image, idol, thing in nature, or fallen angel, mankind will always have a desire for a deity.

"Deity? What deity? I've never seen any deity. I'll believe in a deity when I see one." Sound familiar? You may think this is a good argument against the existence of God, but it's not. As I've said before, there are many different things that you believe in, or put your faith in, that you can't see. Before I referred to microwaves, molecules, and air. But you don't even see your paycheck until you get it in your hand. Yet, you'll spend that money long before you ever lay eyes on that check. You know you've earned that money, so it's as good as yours. The Bible refers to this type of action, or expression of faith, as; "Calling things that be not as though they were." (Romans, chapter 4, verse 17). You may buy something on credit with the intentions of paying it off when you get paid. In other words, you're acting as if you already have the money. You're calling something that is not (the money in your hand) as though it were. You've actually just expressed faith in several things:

#1) That you'll be here to pick up your check on payday.

#2) That the company will actually pay you on payday.

#3) That the check won't bounce when you go to cash it.

Many of us have done this and still do it today. We express faith in many different things without even knowing it. We "take the words" of our friends across town to meet at such and such a place at such and such a time. And without ever seeing those friends, we act in faith, and head for that destination at the designated time. We buy concert tickets fully believing that the performer will show up and play when they're supposed to. We'll even tell all our friends; "I'm going to see so and so in concert." You can't see your friends across town. You can't see that performer heading to your city. And I'll bet most people have never seen the person that cuts their check. So you see, we express faith, or take the words, of people we can't see all the time. So why not express faith, or take the words, of God and His Son Jesus the Christ (Anointed one of God)?

I would hope that the questions that I've raised in this chapter about the Theory of evolution, the time we keep, the names of God and Jesus, the spirit of mankind, and faith in unseen things, has sparked your curiosity. But even if they haven't, I'd like to mention something else to you: physical death.

Each and every one of us must one day face this fact of life. It's not a pleasing subject, but all too real, none the less. You can't run from it and you sure can't hide from it. Whether or not you choose to believe in God the Father, the Son, and the Holy Spirit, has absolutely no bearing at all on their existence. Whether or not you believe in Heaven or Hell has absolutely no bearing at all on their existence. And according to the Bible in Second Corinthians, chapter 5, verse 10; **"We must all appear before the judgement seat of Christ (the Anointed one of God); that everyone may receive the things done in his body, according to that he has done, whether it be good or bad."** You may not believe this statement, but that doesn't make it false. It makes it false to you and that's it. You're entitled to your opinion, but believe it or not, your opinions aren't always right.

Contrary to popular belief, you don't have to wait until you're nearly dead, or in some terrible situation before you call upon the Lord. You can do it at any moment, wherever you may be. How many times have you heard of some prison inmate accepting the Lord? That person didn't have to wait until their life was so messed up before humbling themselves before God.

They could've done it long before they committed that crime. And so can you.

Before I present the opportunity of accepting Jesus the Christ as your Lord and Savior, of which this whole chapter was leading up to, I'll preface it further by saying; this is a personal decision. You can't base it on the "Christians" next door that curse almost every time they open their mouths. You can't base it on the pastor of so and so's church that cheats on his wife with some of the members of his congregation. You can't even base it on the person that goes to church every Sunday morning after a long Saturday night of drinking at the local bar. You can't base it on anyone's actions except those of Jesus. (Take a little time and read Matthew, Mark, Luke, or John, and see what kind of person He really is.) Because only the Godhead (Father, Son, and Holy Spirit) and that particular person knows what lies in their hearts. You could live with someone for twenty years and still not truly know them. One day they could do, or tell you something that is totally opposite of their outward personality. This would most definitely shock you. Why? Because you thought you knew that person. But you really only knew what that person showed or told you. You and I only see or hear what a person wants us to. This may or may not be what truly lies in their heart. The Godhead sees inside and out. So open up your heart and mind and check this out.

#1.)God loves you no matter who you are and no matter what your faults.

A.) Romans 5 : 8

But God commendeth His love toward us, in that, while we were yet sinners, Christ (the Anointed one of God) died for us.

B.) John 3 : 16

For God so loved the world, that He gave His only begotten Son, that whosoever believeth in Him should not perish, but have everlasting life.

#2.)It is Gods' will to save you. You need only have faith in Him and accept His word as truth. Salvation is not something that you can buy or earn.

A.) Ephesians 2 : 8,9

For by grace are ye saved through faith; and that not of yourselves, it is the gift of God: Not of works, lest any man should boast.

#3.)God will not make you accept Him. He awaits your honest invitation.

A.) Revelation 3 : 20

Behold, I stand at the door and knock: if any man hear my voice, and open the door, I will come in to him, and will sup with him, and he with me.

#4.)Gods' only requirement to receiving salvation and spending eternity in His presence is:

A.) Romans 10 : 9,10

That if thou shalt confess with thy mouth the Lord Jesus, and shalt believe in thine heart that God hath raised Him from the dead, thou shalt be saved. For with the heart man believeth unto righteousness; and with the mouth confession is made unto salvation.

B.) 1 John 5 : 11-13

And this is the record, that God hath given us eternal life, and this life is in His Son. He that hath the Son hath life; and he that hath not the Son hath not life. These things have I written unto you that believe on the name of the Son of God; that ye may know that ye have eternal life, and that ye may believe on the name of the Son of God.

I hope that you have decided to accept Jesus as your personal Lord and Savior. I hope that you have opened up your mouth and asked him to come into your heart. Because despite your lot in life, whether the richest, prettiest, strongest, smartest, what have you, one day you will surely die. And at that point it is too late. Not one of us knows a person that has died and returned from the grave to "try it again and do it right the second time around."

Think about it!

FINAL QUESTION

Before asking this final question I'd first like to paint a picture in your mind through the use of this analogy.

Let's say one day you're walking along minding your own business, when you come across a monkey sitting on the side of the road. Well, as soon as you pass this monkey it gets up and starts to follow you. It seems like a friendly little beast. In fact, you've never seen a friendlier looking simian. You and the monkey walk and walk and walk and walk, becoming chummier with every step. After a while the monkey decides that it's too tired to walk anymore. It motions for you to pick it up. You, being the kind person you are, oblige your newfound friend. So, slowly, and ever so gently, it makes its way onto your back. For support, it places its arms snugly around your neck. "Ahhh." you think, "This feels great. You know I could really get used to this. The warmth of its body next to mine. The soft and gentle hug around my neck. This is absolutely fantastic! I think I've found a true friend. Monkey. Don't you ever leave my side. I mean, my back."

Finally you arrive at home. A bit more tired than usual. But you attribute this to getting older rather than your lovable, huggable, free loading new friend. You turn on the television and have a seat. The news is on. They're reporting that

92

thousands, even millions of people support these monkeys on a daily basis. This doesn't surprise you though. Because on your way home you saw quite a few people giving piggy back rides to their own private simians. Some had small ones, like yours, while others had large ones, and still others were toting gorillas around on their backs. The news goes on to give some insight into these hairy beasts....(For the sake of imagination we'll call them Mombozian Snuggle Monkeys.)

The Mombozian Snuggle Monkey starts out small, as we all do. They try to attach themselves to any human that will have them. They have a unique quality in that they grow or shrink in size as their owner's desire for them increases or decreases, respectively. The methods by which people initially bond with them are as diverse as the people who lug them around are. Although some of the most common threads among them seem to be rebellion, escapism, and normalcy (if you will)....

* * * REBELLION * * *

You don't tell me what to do. I'll do whatever I want, whenever I want....Oh, look. There's a cute little monkey. C'mon little monkey. Climb on....Now! Look at me. I'm parading around with a monkey on my back. And there's nothing you can do about it. Ha! Ha! So there.

* * * ESCAPISM * * *

Oh my God! The walls are closing in on me! I need more money! I need more time! I need....Oh look. There's one of those monkeys. C'mon little monkey. Climb on....Aaahhh. What a sensation. Nobody else makes me feel this good. For once I feel appreciated. Problems? What problems? They're all beneath me. I'm flying "high" above 'em all now.

* * * NORMALCY * * *

I don't quite fit in here. I mean, Carol, Bobby, Susan, and Ricky, all have one. And besides that, they've all told me how stupid I look without one. Well...I am in Rome. And damn it! I'm gonna do as the Romans do...Oh look. There's a monkey now. C'mon little monkey. Climb on...Hey! I'm a hep cat now...I've a monkey! They've a monkey! Wouldn't you like to have a monkey too?!

...The news delves deeper into the dangerous and unpredictable nature of these friendly looking creatures. It seems that the so-called snuggle given by the Mombozian Snuggle Monkey is nothing more than a slick diversion set up to get you to lower your defenses. The very nature of the monkey is to seek and destroy. Sometimes, although rarely, it chokes the life out of its victim as soon as it hops aboard. Most times though, it's a slow and steady tightening of its "loving" hug around its victim's neck. So slow, in fact, that in most cases it takes a monkey, ten, twenty, even thirty years or more to dispose of its victim. This constant deprivation of oxygen effects different people in different ways.

The most interesting and amazing fact in dealing with the Mombozian Snuggle Monkey is not so much about the monkey at all. It's his owners, or "victims", shall we say.

You see, in the three examples given earlier; Rebellion, Escapism, and Normalcy, all three of **these owners willingly invited the monkey to come aboard.** And through newscasts like the one you've been watching, and numerous other educational inquiries on the Mombozian Snuggle Monkey; these people knew exactly what they were getting into.

These facts baffle Mombozian Snuggle Monkey researchers far and near. Although the owners know exactly what their fate will be, they go on faithfully toting these wretched beasts around anyway. Then they make up excuses for doing so like; "You've got to go sometime." or, Everybody's going to die of something." or their favorite, "I've been doing this for many many years. These things are totally harmless. Those researchers don't know what the hell they're talking about." Some of them will lie, steal, cheat, or even kill, to keep the so-called "love" of their monkeys. There are centers throughout the world dedicated to studying and possibly curing the seemingly insatiable desire that many humans have for the lovable but deadly Mombozian Snuggle Monkey.

* * * * * *

Well reader. At the beginning of this analogy I said I would first paint a picture in your mind, and then ask a question. Okay. The question is; "If you had a monkey on your back, whether it be a Mombozian Snuggle Monkey or some bad habit (monkey) that you can't seem to shake, and you knew, or at least some reliable source told you that this thing was surely **hindering your full potential in life** and could eventually lead to your death, what exactly will you do?"

Think about it!

Why Not Set Yourself Free?

Right now! You have the ingredients and the power to rid yourself of any unwanted or "bad" habits!

From the day you are born, you face numerous choices.

You hear advice and viewpoints from various voices.

Some say do it. Some say don't.

Some say you will. Some say you won't.

But in this maze of life, with it's many doors.

The choice has always been, and will always be...**yours**.